Isabelle

snowflake

Isabelle raced to the window and looked to the sky

Pointing and smiling
her voice getting high

The first snow of winter had started to fall

All over the ground,
trees, and the wall

Through the flurry of white, the deep unknown

Isabelle spotted a snowflake to call her own

Bubbly and excited
she ran to the door

She wanted to keep her snowflake and gather some more

Dashing outside to the front of her home

Isabelle looked for her snowflake to keep as her own

She looked high in
the trees and under
the bush

She wrapped her scarf around her as she continued to rush

She looked in the plant pots and on the floor

She looked on the walls, the windows and even the door

She looked to the sky through the flurry of snow

The snowflake wasn't there, where must she go?

There were so many snowflakes falling all around

Sadly Isabelle's snowflake was not to be found

Standing in the garden, covered in snow

She smiled, her face,
a rosy glow

She started to
understand, she
started to know

Just one snowflake does not make snow